DAV

THE SO

A MAN OF F

BOOK 3 (TOLD FROM 1 SAMUEL ..., ...

1 CHRONICLES 22)

TOLD BY CARINE MACKENZIE
~ ILLUSTRATED BY GRAHAM KENNEDY ~

COPYRIGHT © 2009 CARINE MACKENZIE
ISBN 978-1-84550-488-5
PUBLISHED BY CHRISTIAN FOCUS PUBLICATIONS, GEANIES HOUSE,
FEARN, TAIN, ROSS-SHIRE, IV20 1TW, SCOTLAND, U.K.
PRINTED IN CHINA

David had been anointed as the future king of Israel by Samuel the prophet. He had to wait patiently until God's time for him to become king.

King Saul and his son Jonathan (David's best friend) were both killed in battle against the Philistines on Mount Gilboa.

When the news came to David, he was very sad. He wept and fasted all day. David wrote a special song of lament which was to be taught to the people.

David then asked God what he should do.

"Go to Hebron," God told him.

David obeyed.

David was anointed king over part of the country – Judah. But one of Saul's sons, Ishbosheth was made king over the rest of the country in defiance of King David.

David had waited patiently for seven and a half years in Hebron. Six sons were born to him then. All this time there was war between David and his followers and Saul's family.

After much fatigue and fighting, Ishbosheth was killed. The men of Israel came to Hebron to ask David to be their king too.

"The Lord has said to you, 'You shall be shepherd of my people Israel,'" they said. So David made a covenant with them and they anointed David as king over Israel too.

This is what he had waited patiently for ever since Saul's death.

King David and his men travelled up to Jerusalem. David lived in the stronghold. He became greater and greater because the Lord was with him.

Hiram, king of Tyre, sent beautiful cedar trees to David at Jerusalem and carpenters and masons who built a house for David.

The ark of the covenant of the Lord was a very important symbol of God's presence with his people. David wanted to take it from Abinadab's house, where it had been for twenty years, to Jerusalem.

Uzzah and Ahio, Abinadab's sons drove a new oxen cart, carrying the ark. But they had forgotten God's instructions about moving the ark. When Uzzah put out his hand to stop the ark falling off the cart, he was struck dead.

David was angry and alarmed. What would he do now?

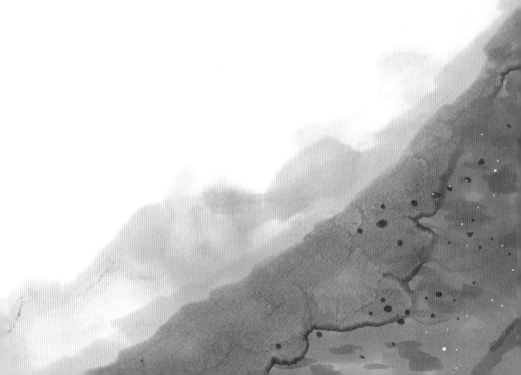

David took the ark aside into Obededom's house. It stayed there for three months. God blessed Obededom and his family.

David decided to move the ark to Jerusalem again. This time it was carried by men appointed by God for these duties. After six steps, David offered a sacrifice to God. The ark of the Lord was brought to Jerusalem with great shouting and rejoicing.

"I have a beautiful cedar house," said David, "but the ark of the Lord is only in a tent. I would like to build a house for God," he told Nathan the prophet.

"You have been a man of war," Nathan told him. "You will not build God's house but your son will."

David was content with making preparations – gathering timber and stone.

David passed on instructions about God's house to his son Solomon.

David and his mighty men continued to win many victories over the Philistines.

David was fair and just in all his dealings with his people.

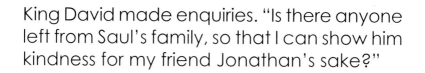

King David made enquiries. "Is there anyone left from Saul's family, so that I can show him kindness for my friend Jonathan's sake?"

"Jonathan's son, Mephibosheth, is still living," David was told.

Mephibosheth was five years old when word came that his father and grandfather had died in battle. His nurse grabbed him up and hurried to escape but she let him fall and as a result he was lame and could not walk.

David invited Mephibosheth to eat at his royal table. He restored Saul's land to him. David showed him kindness for his father Jonathan's sake. He had not forgotten the covenant that he had made with Jonathan long ago.

David waited patiently for God's timing in many difficulties and adventures. His desire was to commit his way to the Lord and to trust in him to do all things well. You can read about that in Psalm 37.

This is good advice for us too.